QuikStep GUIDES FOR BUSY MANAGERS

# QuikStep FIRING

## STEP BY STEP THROUGH MANAGEMENT'S MOST DIFFICULT TASK

BY STEPHEN D. BRUCE, PH.D.

RANSOM & BENJAMIN PUBLISHERS LLC

## Credits

| | |
|---|---|
| Legal Editor: | Dorit Heimer, J.D.<br>Levett, Rockwood & Sanders, P.C., Westport, CT |
| Copy Editor: | Kathleen S. Marshall |
| Production Editor: | Abigail J. Bruce |



ISBN Number 0-9645093-6-9

Printed in the United States of America



Substantial quantity discounts available from the publisher.

Comments or questions? Please contact Ransom & Benjamin Publishers LLC

P.O. Box 160, Mystic, CT 06355, PH 860-536-2000, FAX 860-536-1545.

*This publication is designed to provide accurate and authoritative information in regard to the subject matter covered. It is sold with the understanding that the publisher is not engaged in rendering legal, accounting or other professional services. If legal advice or other expert assistance is required, the services of a competent professional should be sought.—From a Declaration of Principles jointly adopted by a Committee of the American Bar Association and a Committee of Publishers.*

# Table of Contents

# INTRODUCTION

If you are like most managers, terminating an employee—even when fully justified—is the most difficult, or at least the most unpleasant, responsibility you face.

## CAN THIS BOOK MAKE FIRING FUN?

Can this book make firing fun? No, sorry about that. Firing employees will never be a pleasant part of your job. However, the steps outlined in this book can make it a manageable responsibility that you can carry out with dignity and consideration. As you follow the steps below, you will accomplish:

- ☛ an investigation that will give you the confidence to know that termination is the right thing to do.
- ☛ a legal analysis that will insure that you don't create a major lawsuit that could have been avoided.
- ☛ a termination plan that will help you to know that you are doing it the best way it can be done.

No, it won't be fun; but it will be completed quickly and efficiently, in a way you can be proud of and which will cause the least discomfort for the person being terminated.

## YOU ARE NOT READY ... YET

Are you are reading this book because you want to fire an employee?

Stop right there.

Until you have completed the first three steps outlined below, think of the situation as a *possible* termination. As you will see, there are many reasons why firing an employee might not be in the organization's best interests.

## ALWAYS SEEK HR GUIDANCE

Always check with the your human resources department for guidance before you terminate an employee. Federal and state laws, organization policy and practice, and a host of other important considerations must be considered before any action is taken.

## HOW THIS BOOK WILL HELP

The steps in this book are designed to do three things:

**1. Break the firing process down into manageable segments.** Step-by-step procedures ensure that all the bases are covered.

**2. Help you to perform a legal termination.** You want to accomplish a termination that will stand up in court, and you do not want to create more legal problems than you had when you started.

**3. Give you the knowledge you need.** Careful explanations of all the issues ensure that you know what to do, how to do it, and, especially important, what not to do.

**4. Give you the tools you need.** This book shows how to handle every step of the way. Sample statements, checklists, and expert tips make for a calm and rational termination, which reduces the employee's discomfort and your anxiety.

## FOR CAUSE AND NO-FAULT TERMINATIONS

There are many reasons for terminations; however, for purposes of this book, it is useful to think of no-fault and for cause terminations.

## TERMINATIONS TRIGGER LAWSUITS

Terminations trigger the vast majority of employee lawsuits. Most of them could have been avoided by following a few simple rules.

Follow the steps outlined in this book. Answer the key questions the book presents. Then you will be able to make a considered decision that will stand up in court.

### No-Fault or situational terminations

No-fault terminations are cases such as layoffs, reductions in force, eliminations of jobs or departments, etc. Often these terminations do not reflect poorly on the employee at all. You can provide an enthusiastic reference, and you can support the employee in finding a new position.

In other cases, the poorer performers may have been let go, and the termination may to some extent reflect the employee's performance. Yet, you probably will still be able to give a good recommendation and provide assistance.

In these no-fault terminations, the first steps in this book—investigation and legal review—may been done already by the organization's human resource experts. However, careful planning and detailed attention to the termination meeting are still necessary.

### 'For cause' terminations

These terminations stem from either major performance problems or serious violations of the organization's rules or policies.

In most organizations, such offenses might include:

☛ inability to perform up to standards despite training and coaching.

☛ repeat violations of attendance or tardiness rules.

☛ breaking rules against fighting or stealing.

☛ engaging in behaviors such as sexual harassment.

Naturally, it is these "for cause" terminations that create the greatest difficulty for managers. They also form the basis for the most lawsuits.

Especially because of that fact, even if you are sure that your termination is legitimate and the best way to deal with the situation, go through all the steps outlined in this book.

Why? First, there may be a good reason—often one that you could not know about—for reconsidering a termination.

Second, if you do terminate, you will know (and you will be able to show a jury) that you evaluated the situation rationally and carefully and made a reasoned decision.

## REDUCE THE NUMBER OF TERMINATIONS

If terminations make you uncomfortable, think about things you might change in your management style to reduce the number of terminations. What is the number one thing you can do? Be much more careful about whom you hire. When you put the right person in the right job, you won't have to fire very often.

If, however, you are careless in your hiring, you'll end up with troublemakers, and people who are not right for their jobs. That's a termination waiting to happen.

What is the key to good hiring? Know what you are looking for, and design a hiring process that will enable you to determine who meets your requirements.

Then, do in-depth reference and background checks to weed out troublemakers and malcontents.

## IT'S ALL FOR THE BEST

It is not easy to convince someone who has just been fired that everything is going to work out for the best. In fact, later on in this book, we warn against trying to do that. Nevertheless, the truth is that most fired employees do find new jobs, and many find jobs that pay better and offer more opportunity. Even if the employee can't appreciate this right away, it will be helpful if you do.

# STEP 1

## STOP, LISTEN, AND LOOK

**GOALS FOR STEP 1**

✔*Stop the action before you do something you will regret.*

✔*Listen to the employee's side of the story.*

✔*Look into the situation—Conduct an investigation if necessary.*

Never take firing an employee lightly.

Acting too quickly, without thinking the situation through and seeking advice, can be dangerous.

In fact, from a legal standpoint, terminations are the most dangerous acts of management. Most of the big-dollar lawsuits come from employees who have been fired. And many of those lawsuits could have been avoided if the managers involved had backed off and taken time to consider the situation carefully .

Stop, listen, and look before acting.

# STOP—SUSPEND THE ACTION

No matter what the offense, final action is not immediately required. You always have time to back off, investigate, reflect, and seek advice.

## IS IMMEDIATE ACTION NECESSARY?

Some situations seem to demand immediate action. For example, employees have been openly insubordinate, broken important rules like fighting or stealing, or forgotten to ship an order you promised to your best customer. Or maybe they just reached "the last straw" in your progressive discipline system.

In these situations, you may be tempted to "be a real manager" and "do what has to be done."

You are angry (and the anger may be justified), but that is not the frame of mind to be in when making critical employment decisions.

Acting on the spur of the moment often leads to ill-considered decisions, irresponsible public humiliation of an employee, or other lawsuit-provoking behavior.

When that behavior costs the organization $100,000 in legal fees, how far do you think your excuse, "Well, gosh, I was angry," will get you?

## WHY A DELAY IS IMPORTANT

Delaying action is important for reasons beyond emotion and anger.

- ☛ First of all, managers often don't know precisely what the appropriate action is in a given circumstance. A colleague or an HR representative, however, may be able to put a broader perspective on the situation, and ensure that it is handled consistently according to organization policy.

- ☛ In addition, most managers aren't familiar with all the legal issues. There are may legal issues which involve terminations. For example, has the employee in question:
  - —asked for family leave?
  - become disabled or announced a pregnancy?
  - —had a talk with OSHA about problems in the plant, or made any formal complaint to a government agency?

If any of these things have happened, the termination might be viewed as retaliation.

- ☛ **Other activity.** In addition, there may be other personnel actions taking place of which the manager may not be aware. For example, reductions in force, reassignments, or restructurings could be planned that would affect the decision.
- ☛ **Group decision.** It is generally in the organization's best interest for termination decisions to be made by a group.

(Note: These legal issues are detailed in the next chapter.)

## HOW TO DELAY ACTION

You don't have to give up your management rights because you have chosen—wisely—to delay action. You may delay, and still discuss a situation, impose discipline, or terminate.

For example, you might say:

*"I'd like to see you in my office at three, and we'll discuss this matter."*

*"I'll be speaking with each of you individually before the end of the day."*

*"It's clear that we have a serious problem here. I want to reflect on the situation, and I will talk to you tomorrow."*

A more serious step, but one which still preserves your ability to take the time to make a good decision is a suspension with pay.

This removes the person from the action, and allows you to investigate, confer, do whatever is necessary before making a decision. (This action is discussed in more detail in the third chapter.)

## LISTEN—GIVE THE EMPLOYEE A CHANCE TO EXPLAIN

Make sure the employee has a chance to explain. There are two important reasons for this.

First, should the employee sue, and you end up in front of a jury, you won't have to face an accusation that you "never even gave the poor employee a chance to explain."

Second, you would like to have the employee's explanation on record right away, so that later on he or she won't be able to concoct a fictional, but perhaps believable, story for the jury.

If the employee's explanation may offer sufficient excuse for the behavior, you probably want to investigate further to establish the truth.

## LOOK—GATHER THE FACTS

Once you have stopped the action, and listened to the employee's side of the story, take the time to verify the facts that are leading you to consider termination.

### WHEN YOU SHOULD INVESTIGATE

Investigation is a step required when you need to determine whether the action prompting the termination actually happened, or when facts are in dispute. It may also be wise in certain other cases, to show that the organization was acting responsibly, and give the employee the benefit of the doubt.

## WHEN YOU MIGHT NOT INVESTIGATE

In some cases, however, little or no investigation may be necessary—or desirable. For example, if you have clearly established that the employee has committed an offense for which termination is the company's standard response, you may not have to investigate any farther. Such situations might include:

- an employee admits to having stolen valuable company property, or was caught trying to sneak it out of the facility.
- an employee threatened other employees with a gun and there were many witnesses.
- an employee has been on a program of progressive discipline and has reached the end of the line.

In these cases, when there is no dispute as to the facts of the situation and company policy provides for termination, a limited investigation will probably suffice. You just need to investigate far enough to be sure that the alleged offense really happened.

### INFORMATION YOU DON'T WANT

Generally, if you have good grounds to terminate for poor performance, or breaking an established rule, you may want to limit your investigation because you don't want to know any additional information.

Say, for example, a performance problem warrants an employee's termination. You could terminate on that basis; however, you decide to conduct a thorough investigation. During the investigation, you turn up the fact that the employee has had drug and alcohol problems. Now you have to consider the question of whether the employee is disabled and entitled to a reasonable accommodation. Termination based on the performance problem would have avoided that issue.

## KEY QUESTIONS BEFORE YOU INVESTIGATE

Answer these questions before you begin an in-depth investigation.

### Do you need attorney-client privilege?

If you conduct your investigation without consulting your attorney, the results of the investigation are likely to be subject to "discovery." That is, you may be required to disclose the results in the event of a lawsuit.

In fact, in some cases, information contained in an employer's investigation has provided a blue print for a successful suit against the employer.

However, if your attorney directs the investigation, you may be able to keep the results confidential because of the attorney-client privilege.

If you want this protection, contact your attorney as soon as possible; otherwise, the privilege will probably be lost.

### Who will conduct your investigation?

Investigations may be conducted by the managers involved, representatives of the HR department, or members of the security team. Or, as mentioned above, attorneys and outside investigators may also be used.

### When should you investigate?

Once you decide to investigate, the quicker the better. The longer you wait, the more likely that memories will dim, stories will change, witnesses will compare notes, and evidence will be moved or disappear.

### What methods will your investigation require?

In addition to interviewing those involved and witnesses, you may wish to use other sources of information, for example:

- ❑ Records, logs, diaries
- ❑ Videotapes
- ❑ Surveillance
- ❑ Searches
- ❑ Physical evidence

**Whom should you interview?**

You want to balance the need to be thorough with the need to maintain confidentiality and the need to keep interruptions and productivity loss to a minimum.

In the first round, talk to witnesses or others with direct involvement. If they refer you to others who can likely offer more information— information you need—then follow the trail another round.

## PREPARE A QUESTION OUTLINE

Before you start interviewing witnesses, make up a list of questions. A consistent set of questions makes it easier to compare answers, and helps ensure that you don't forget any important questions.

However, each witness may have a unique contribution to make, so as you interview, tailor your questions as necessary, and don't hesitate to probe a little deeper if necessary.

## INVESTIGATORY INTERVIEWING

Here are some general guidelines for good investigative interviews:

- ☛ Remain objective. Treat complaints as valid until you establish otherwise.
- ☛ Treat each incident separately.
- ☛ Maintain a need-to-know basis—limit access to information.
- ☛ Do not unnecessarily disclose information to witnesses.

- ☛ Maintain confidence, but do not promise confidentiality.
- ☛ Try to not involve witnesses whom you doubt will maintain confidentiality.
- ☛ Inform the witness that the investigation is confidential. Inform current employees that a breach of confidentiality will result in disciplinary action. *Important: Failure to keep the investigation confidential can lead to defamation or invasion of privacy claims.*

**In interviewing the employee:**

- ❑ Review the situation which may result in termination.
- ❑ Determine the employee's side of the story.
- ❑ Get specific details of the incident(s).
- ❑ Determine whether or not there were witnesses to the incident(s).
- ❑ Determine whether or not the employee spoke to anyone else about the incident(s).

**In interviewing witnesses:**

- ❑ Remain objective.
- ❑ Determine whether or not the witness observed the situation.
- ❑ Phrase questions so as not to give unnecessary information. For example, say "Were you present in the executive suite at noon on February 12 ... what did you see?" rather than, "Did you see where Jack mercilessly beat up John and threw the desk through the office window?"
- ❑ Determine or confirm when and where the incident occurred.
- ❑ Determine in detail what happened, who was standing where, who did what to whom, and so on.
- ❑ Determine what other witnesses were present.
- ❑ Determine whether or not the employee has spoken to anyone else about the incident(s).

Take careful notes as you interview so you will remember for sure who said what.

## OBTAIN OTHER NEEDED INFORMATION

There are additional pieces of information you will need in order to make your termination decision.

### Employee's record

You would like to know what sort of employee this individual has been. How long has he or she been employed, what have performance reviews said, what promotions or positives are in the file, and what negatives or past discipline is recorded in the file.

### What organization rules and policies apply

Find out what policies and organization rules apply to this situation. If the employee is accused of breaking a rule, find out where the rule is stated, and how the employee would have known about it. If a policy covers the situation, find out what the policy states with respect to this particular situation.

### What action has been taken in other similar situations

If there have been similar situations in the past, find out what actions were taken with those employees.

# QUIKCHECK

## ARE YOU READY?

- ❑ Action has been delayed to allow time to consider.
- ❑ The employee has been given a chance to explain.
- ❑ Consideration has been given to NOT investigating.
- ❑ The need for attorney-client privilege has been considered.
- ❑ Investigation planning (who, when, what, how) is completed.
- ❑ Investigation is completed.
- ❑ Additional information is assembled, including employee records, organization rules and policies, and records of actions taken in similar situations.

# STEP 2

# AUDIT FOR LEGALITY AND FAIRNESS

**GOALS FOR STEP 2**

✔*Determine whether you have behaved legally.*
✔*Determine whether you have behaved fairly.*
✔*Understand how to document a termination.*

More lawsuits arise out of terminations than any other employee action. So, once you have completed Step 1 and you have a clear picture of the situation, you must go through a series of questions to be sure that you are not risking a lawsuit.

In some cases, legal restraints may even preclude a termination, for example, when an employment contract prevents such action.

In other cases, the likelihood of a successful lawsuit may suggest that another approach rather than termination would be better.

For example, in the case in which management has just been notified that the employee in question has filed a discrimination claim with the Equal Employment Opportunity Commission (EEOC), and the employee's performance reviews are satisfactory, termination may look like retaliation.

Go over the questions below carefully. If there is any question about going ahead, delay action until you can work out the answers.

### What is the difference between legality and fairness?

As many organizations have found to their dismay, just being technically legal is often not enough. Juries often react more on the basis of fairness than of law. And, from a morale standpoint, so do the rest of your employees. Therefore, it is necessary to evaluate both the actual legal requirements, and the softer issue of fairness.

# HAVE YOU BEHAVED LEGALLY?

First, determine whether the planned termination will be a legal action.

## HAVE YOU FOLLOWED YOUR OWN POLICIES?

Most organizations have a discipline policy that covers termination. Check your policy to be sure that you have followed it, especially if your policy calls for "progressive discipline" or suggests that employees are only fired for cause.

The power of progressive discipline is that with the clear series of warnings given along the way, and with agreements to improve having been made, it is clear to everyone (including the jury) that the organization has given the employee a fair chance.

Policies generally reserve the right to skip steps in the progressive discipline system and fire immediately for certain offenses such as stealing or violence. However, you should exercise this right with caution.

## IS THERE A CONTRACT OR OTHER GUARANTEE?

The next step is to determine whether this termination would violate a written or implied employment contract or other similar guarantee.

### Written employment contracts

If the employee in question has a written contract covering your employment relationship, you will probably be bound by the terms of the contract. An offer letter that details employment arrangements might be considered as a contract as well.

If there is a contract, does it limit your right to terminate? Under what circumstances?

If, for example, you may only terminate for cause, then you need to have the evidence to back up your position.

### Implied contracts

Many courts have found that certain documents, such as employee handbooks, can create implied employment contracts. For example, if your handbook contains statements that could be interpreted as guaranteeing a job as long as work is satisfactory, check to be sure that your documentation backs up your position that work was not satisfactory. If your handbook guarantees or could be interpreted as guaranteeing some kind of progressive discipline steps, check to be sure that you have followed the provisions.

### Policy guarantees

Are there policy guarantees to which you must adhere?

Check your employee handbook and personnel policies for guarantees which might conflict with your decision to terminate.

Do any provisions require arbitration or other alternate dispute resolution approaches?

### Statements by management

Has management made any statements to the individual (for example, during the hiring process) that indicate a guarantee of continued employment? Have such statements been made at annual gatherings? Be sure that your termination action is sound within the bounds of such statements.

### Union agreements

Is the employee in question covered by a union contract? Would this termination be contrary to union contract provisions?

In a unionized organization, a variety of clauses in the union contract may govern or impact the ways in which you may discipline or terminate your employees. For example, employees may have the right to be accompanied by a union representative during a disciplinary meeting.

In a unionized situation, consult with HR before taking serious actions affecting employees.

Has the employee been involved in union organizing? Could the offense for which the employee might be terminated be considered "concerted activity"? Again, consult with the HR department.

## COULD THIS FIRING BE VIEWED AS DISCRIMINATORY?

Many termination lawsuits allege discrimination. In such cases, a terminated employee claims that he or she was fired not for the reason the organization states, but because of discrimination. (You fired me because I am [old, black, disabled, etc.], not because I broke the rule.)

To counter this argument, you need to show that your behavior was consistent with similar situations in the past, and that it was for the business reason you state.

### Have you been consistent?

Consistent treatment is an important part of non-discriminatory treatment. If you have consistently terminated others for the same offense that you now want to terminate someone for, you are probably going to be all right. If, however, you have never terminated a white male for an offense which has occurred frequently, and now you intend to terminate your only black male for that offense, you are on very thin ice.

**Do you have a well-documented business reason?**

Generally, if you can support a well-documented business reason for your actions—for example, poor performance—you are more likely to win the lawsuit.

☛Do you have adequate documentation?

In many of these cases, there's a problem—lack of good documentation.

You say the employee was terminated for poor performance, yet your documents or actions indicate that the employee's performance was good.

This problem is usually a result of performance appraisal "inflation." That is, when the manager gives almost everyone satisfactory or better ratings.

☛Tell it to the jury

Imagine yourself—on the witness stand—explaining that a termination was due to incompetence or poor production or attitude, or whatever. Then the defense attorney produces a string of performance appraisals—signed by you—that say "satisfactory," or "good." Case closed. No matter what you say now, you appear to be lying. Your poor performance argument now appears to be a fabrication or pretense.

☛Actions may speak as loudly as words

Sometimes, it doesn't even take a formal document to show acceptable performance. Just the fact that you treated the employee like other good-performing employees, that is, gave raises and bonuses, is enough to convince a jury that you are lying about the poor performance.

**On what basis may an employee be protected?**

Here are bases on which employees may be protected. If any apply to your situation, step back and take a careful look at the context of your actions.

Note: not all apply in every state or locale. If there is any question, check with your human resources department.

☛Race or National Origin

☛Creed or Religion

☛Sex

☛Age

☛Marital Status

☛Sexual Orientation

☛Disability

If you base a termination decision—in whole or in part—on whether or not someone has a disability, you are begging for a lawsuit. Some of the obvious disabilities may include:

- ❑ Blindness
- ❑ Deafness
- ❑ Alcoholism
- ❑ AIDS
- ❑ Mental incapacities
- ❑ Stress
- ❑ Back pain

Other health problems which may be more problematic to identify as disabilities include illegal drug use and being overweight.

Understanding what is and is not a disability is one of the toughest problems managers face. And the requirements for "reasonable accommodation" of disabilities are just about as tough.

The law provides protection in certain circumstances and not in others—check with your HR department when you encounter disabilities.

### ☛Pregnancy

In general, treat pregnant women the same way you treat any other employee with a disability. This means that you may not fire a woman because she is pregnant.

### ☛Various State-Law-Based Prohibitions

Most states have their own laws prohibiting various types of discrimination. For example, sexual orientation, child-bearing capacity, public assistance status, off-duty smoking, and filing of a workers' compensation claim may be protected behaviors or categories in your state.

## How managers discriminate

Discrimination comes in many forms, some obvious and overt, some subtle and hard to spot. Here's what to avoid during terminations:

### ☛Overt discrimination (I don't like X's)

This is the out-in-the-open type of discrimination that most people think of when they hear the word. For example:

I fired Terry because I don't like to work with [women, old people, black people, disabled people].

I fired Sue because my customers don't like to deal with [men, white people, Asian people].

I don't think [old people, Asian people, pregnant women] can do this type of job.

☛Stereotypes (X's can't X)

Stereotyping usually takes the form of "X's can't X." For example:

Women just aren't strong enough for these jobs.

☛Patronize/paternalize/maternalize (X's shouldn't X)

This is a special form of stereotyping that seems well-intentioned, but is, in general, discriminatory. For example, "We have to let her go; she has a young child now and she shouldn't travel."

☛Play favorites (I won't fire my friends)

Managers may have friends at work. They always get the plum projects, and they never seem to be the ones who get fired.

☛Reverse Discrimination

Reverse discrimination means discriminating against someone as a result of your attempts not to discriminate against someone else. This could be a problem, for example, if you fire a white male to keep a black female.

## COULD THIS FIRING BE VIEWED AS RETALIATION FOR EXERCISING A GUARANTEED RIGHT?

Has the employee in question filed any complaints recently, or exercised any other employee rights?

Terminating an employee for exercising any of these rights may be viewed as illegal retaliation.

### Rights guaranteed by law

Among the rights that employees enjoy by law are the following:

☛Civic duties

— the right to vote.

— the right to perform jury duty.

— in some states, the right to answer a subpoena to testify in court.

☛**Safe workplace**

— the right to a safe workplace environment (under the Occupational Safety and Health Act or similar state acts).

— the right to report unsafe situations in the workplace without retaliation.

☛**Illegal actions**

— the right not to perform an illegal act. For example, a worker who refuses to falsify testimony or participate in a price-fixing scheme may be protected from termination.

— the right to report illegal activity (engage in whistleblowing) without retaliation.

☛**Uphold the public interest**

— in some states, the right to act in the public interest. Workers who are doing the "right thing," even though there may be no specific law protecting their action, may be protected from termination.

☛**Legal activities outside of work**

— in some states, the right to engage in legal activities outside of work. Although many of these laws were passed to prohibit employers from discriminating against smokers, they may also protect other social activities.

☛**Garnishment**

— the right not to be disciplined as a result of having had one's pay garnished, that is, reduced by an amount that the employer is ordered to pay to someone else as a result of a court order.

☛**Medical leave**

— the right to unpaid leave in certain circumstances (for example, under the Family and Medical Leave Act).

☛Disability accommodation

— the right to have disabilities accommodated within reason (under the Americans with Disabilities Act).

☛Workers' Compensation

— the right to file workers' compensation claims after an accident or injury without retaliation.

☛Freedom from harassment

— the right to treatment free from illegal harassment. An employee who has reported harassment, but the harassment continues, may resign but claim "constructive discharge."

☛Union activity

— the right to participate in certain union activities (under the National Labor Relations Act).

Special rules apply to unionized organizations. Any manager or supervisor operating in a union-organized facility or who deals with organized employees must be trained in the rules that govern the management/worker relationship, and must be thoroughly familiar with the union contract and how its provisions are interpreted.

Talk to the HR department before terminating a union employee.

Even in non-unionized organizations, there are certain rights that employees have in organizing. If you want to terminate an employee who may have been engaging in union-organizing activity, contact the HR department.

☛Political activity

— in some states, the right to engage in certain political activity.

☛Compensation

— the right to pay and overtime according to certain rules (under the Fair Labor Standards Act).

— the right to make complaints about wage and hour issues without retaliation.

— the right to be paid within certain time frames and to be given details of pay and deductions.

☛Benefits

— under the Employee Retirement and Income Security Act (ERISA), certain rights pertaining to pensions and other benefits. For example, employees have the right not to be terminated just so the employer can avoid providing a benefit, such as vesting in a pension plan.

The subject of benefits is highly technical; you should seek expert guidance for any such questions.

☛Veterans' rights

Veterans enjoy special rights, including leave for certain military service and the right to return to work under certain circumstances.

**Rights that may be assumed**

Other employee rights may not be direct legal rights, but are often implied or assumed to be rights by a court or a jury.

☛Right to be treated with dignity

During the termination process, avoid any behavior that would degrade or humiliate an employee. Do not act with explosive anger, rage, or violence.

☛Right to 'good faith and fair dealing'

Would a termination violate an average person's view of good faith? Some courts may recognize an obligation on the part of the employer to deal with employees at a reasonable level of good faith, regardless of whether any particular laws actually require this level of treatment.

For example, did you uproot an employee and family to move to a new job and then fire the employee two months later?

☛Right to privacy

Observe privacy rights in dealing with terminations.

Generally, employees have few privacy rights at work, especially if your policies so state. However, privacy rights may be assumed for areas like desks, file cabinets, lockers, and cars. It is always best to have reasonable cause to invade an employee's privacy.

You would be wise to consult with the HR department or other experts before launching an investigation, monitoring, surveillance, and other such activity, as both federal and state laws probably apply.

In conducting an investigation, you probably should ask permission to search. If your organization has a policy requiring cooperation with searches and investigations, you may discipline any employee who refuses the search.

## Never retaliate

Every manager is annoyed or angered from time to time by an employee exercising legally guaranteed rights—what manager wants to lose a good worker for 12 weeks of leave or likes being reported to a government agency? Retaliation may come to mind: "I'll fix that so-and-so."

Don't retaliate. It is an invitation to a lawsuit. And retaliation will never help your case—it will always seem unfair.

As with so many personnel actions, watch appearances. Don't take action that might appear to be retaliation; it can be hard to prove your true motives. For example, terminating an employee the day after he or she reports a safety violation to OSHA may be a poor idea—no matter how deserved the termination.

# HAVE YOU BEHAVED FAIRLY?

In addition to making a strict legal analysis of the situation, it is wise to also ask the more general question, "has the company treated this individual fairly?"

## THINK THE WAY A JURY THINKS

Although judges carefully instruct jury members in the finer points of law involved in their cases, the truth is that juries are generally swayed more by a desire for fairness than by a desire for technical legal correctness.

Juries ask this question:

*Was the employer fair to the employee?*

And if they believe it was not, the jury asks:

*What can we do to remedy the situation?*

And sometimes, they get to ask a third question:

*How can we punish the employer so this won't happen again?*

For instance, let's say your company promises a long-time employee something, then doesn't deliver and fires the employee. The employee sues. Your company argues that it had no legal obligation. The employee says simply, I trusted your company—the company where I gave my all for 20 years—and its actions weren't fair.

Your company may be technically right, but with whom do you think the jury will side? The big, bad, deep-pockets employer who treated a long-term employee shabbily? Or the poor, long-suffering, hard-working employee?

### What does a jury think fairness means?

To avoid actions that generate lawsuits, think like a jury member—think fairness as you deal with your employees. When the jury asks, was the employer fair, you want their answer to be, yes, it was.

Read through these questions a jury member might be asking about the termination you are considering:

- ❑ Did the employee know what the employer expected of her?
- ❑ Did he know what consequences could result from his actions?
- ❑ Did the employee get what was promised to her?
- ❑ Did a manager take action before finding out the facts?
- ❑ Was the same action taken as was taken in similar circumstances in the past?
- ❑ Were the decision criteria fair?
- ❑ Were policies and rules followed?
- ❑ Did the employee have a chance to explain?
- ❑ Did the manager or organization trick or deceive the employee in any way?
- ❑ Did the manager "kick the employee while he was down"?

**Would your termination be consistent with past behavior?**

As mentioned above, consistency is an important element of fairness. Consistency means that for any given set of facts or circumstances, your actions toward similar employees are the same.

For example, if you terminate one employee for missing the third day in a row without calling in, but then don't terminate the next employee who fails to call by the third day, you're setting up an unfair situation. If that employee turns around and complains that you did this because he or she is a member of a protected group, will you be able to support your decision? It won't be easy if you haven't been consistent.

**Would your termination be reasonable?**

Reasonableness means that a reasonable, neutral observer would find your action within the bounds of normal behavior.

For example, for a minor infraction, did you discharge a long-time, loyal employee? "That doesn't seem fair" is what the jury will think, even if you and your lawyer are thinking "this is an employment-at-will firm and we can fire whomever we want whenever we want."

### Is the employee a long-term employee?

Is the employee being considered for termination a long-term employee? In general, courts expect long-term employees to be given a little more leniency than short-term employees. Whenever you are considering firing a long-term employee, take a special look at the situation.

## Is Documentation in Order?

To ensure a legally secure termination, you should have complete documentation to back up your action.

When there's no record of misbehavior or unsatisfactory performance, and no record of having talked to the employee about it, it's hard to suggest that misbehavior was a problem. Especially if there is a record of "satisfactory" performance ratings, there's little you can do to convince anyone that there was a performance problem.

In the face of a lawsuit alleging discrimination, you're going to look silly with no notes, no dates, no proof. Here is what your employee's attorney will be asking:

"You took the time and trouble to make a written record of the satisfactory behavior every six months (the performance appraisal), and you're trying to tell us that there was unsatisfactory behavior, for which you didn't even take the time to make a record, that was bad enough to warrant termination?"

## TYPICAL DOCUMENTATION

Documentation would typically be used to prove that an employee:

- ❑ was given a warning.
- ❑ committed certain acts at certain times.
- ☑ knew of a certain rule or expectation.
- ❑ received particular training.
- ❑ received a copy of the employee handbook.
- ❑ broke company rules at certain times and dates.
- ❑ received certain levels of warnings and discipline.
- ❑ was placed on some type of probationary status.

If you have documented your actions and observations, you can prove what took place.

### How to keep your records

For documentation to be most effective, it should be detailed, accurate, and current.

#### ☛Detailed

Record in some detail what took place. For example, a note such as "discussed Joe's performance with him" is much weaker and more vague than a listing of specific instances with specific recommendations for improvement. Be sure to do the following:

- ❑ Note dates, times, places, witnesses, etc.
- ❑ Record what the employee is expected to do in response.
- ❑ Record what you will do if the employee fails to respond or improve.

#### ☛Accurate

Be sure that all that you write is accurate. If any part of your document is proven wrong, the validity of the entire document is called into question.

☛Current

Write your memo at the time the event occurs, and be sure to date it. Such "contemporaneous" records carry much more weight than those created after the fact, which often appear more like fabrication than documentation.

### Critical incidents diary

The groundwork for discipline and termination is often laid well before the actual progressive discipline system kicks in. For example, an employee may have been warned informally several times before the first formal warning is issued under the discipline system.

Unfortunately, these early warnings are often not documented. Some experts recommend that managers keep a diary of critical incidents, both good and bad, on a daily basis. Then you'll have a record of those early warnings and counseling sessions to bolster your basis for termination.

### What does a document prove?

Will my notes be accepted in court?

If you can show that your documentation is consistent and reliable, your written word, recorded at the time of an action, is likely to be accepted as true.

Furthermore, it's far better than no documentation at all.

## NEVER FALSIFY A DOCUMENT

Never falsify, backdate, or alter any document. First of all, it is not likely that you can get away with it; second, the penalties will be severe; and third, you're likely to lose your case.

In court, once you are proven to have lied once, your credibility is gone.

## DON'T BUILD A 'PAPER CASE'

When you want to fire an employee, but the record shows satisfactory performance, or contains no hint of problems, someone may suggest to you that you start "building a case" against the problem employee by documenting everything the employee does wrong. This action surely will increase your evidence of poor performance and will help you to support termination.

Unfortunately, however, there's a dangerous trap here. If you focus on documenting only one employee's shortcomings, or if you document trivial infractions, that could end up helping to prove a claim of discrimination. It will certainly appear that the employee was singled out for this "special" treatment, and that you were "out to get" the employee.

It's better to follow the rule of consistency—when infractions occur, write them up for every employee who commits them, not just one.

# QUIKCHECK

## HAVE YOU ACTED LEGALLY AND FAIRLY?

- ❑ Have you followed your policies?
- ❑ Is there a contract or other guarantee?
- ❑ Will any laws be violated?
- ❑ Could this act be viewed as discrimination?
- ❑ Could this act be viewed as retaliation against an employee for exercising a right?
- ❑ Have you behaved fairly?
- ❑ Will a termination in this situation be consistent with your actions in similar situations in the past?
- ❑ Is your documentation in order?

# STEP 3

## MAKE A GROUP DECISION

**GOALS FOR STEP 3**

✔*Learn why a group decision is needed for a termination.*
✔*Understand when to consider an alternative course of action.*
✔*See what factors to consider for a final determination.*

Even if you're sure you know what to do, it's often better to act from a group decision. Here's why.

- **Consult the experts.** First of all, other members of your management team—for example, the human resource manager—may be in a better position to determine the most appropriate reaction because they are familiar with the actions the organization has taken in similar circumstances. In addition, they are trained to interpret organization policy and employment law.
- **Power of a group decision.** But there is another important reason: if the action you are taking should ever be ques-

tioned in court, a group decision will demonstrate that the decision was arrived at by careful consideration. The decision of a single manager may well be viewed as self-serving, emotional, or discriminatory, where the decision of a group will be more likely to appear reasoned and businesslike.

- **The need for witnesses.** Furthermore, since litigation can go on for years, and since managers come and go, it's in the organization's best interest to have several managers familiar with the particulars of a situation. Otherwise, when a case comes to trial, the only management witness may be long gone.

# Is Termination the Best Alternative?

The next question to ask is this: is termination the best solution or are there less drastic alternatives?

Even when you are sure that termination is the answer, consider the question. If a lawsuit develops, you can be sure that the jury will want to know whether you considered suspension or some other less drastic measure.

## CONSIDER OTHER ALTERNATIVES TO TERMINATION

Here are some alternatives to consider:

### Suspensions without pay

In many organizations, the final step before an employee is fired is a suspension—without pay—for perhaps three or even five days. The intent is to remind the employee forcefully that the work problems are indeed serious. Generally, if there is a repeat of the problem within a specified period of time after the suspension, the employee is fired.

Note that you must be careful with exempt employees and unpaid suspensions; you might lose the exemption if you do not follow strict rules. Check with your human resources department.

### Suspensions with pay

Some employers are modifying the standard practice of suspension without pay—they pay the worker during the suspension and stress the employee's empowerment in making decisions related to his or her future at the company.

Variously called a decision-making leave or a personal commitment day, the practice offers a day's leave during which the problem employee must determine whether he or she is going to come back and meet the employer's work requirements or leave the organization.

This provides a documented, final wake-up call for an errant employee. You've talked, you've had coaching sessions, you've given written warnings—all of which have failed. The paid suspension is a dramatic gesture that says, unmistakably, the end is at hand. It also makes it perfectly clear that the employee knew the situation was serious, and that the organization did all it could to give the employee a chance.

The jury's reaction will be: This company really was fair!

### Resignation

Will the circumstances permit the employee to "resign"?

Sometimes, this solution is a "win-win" all around. It allows the employee to preserve dignity and move into a job search without the stigma of having been fired. And it allows the employer to reduce (not eliminate) the likelihood of a lawsuit.

You don't eliminate lawsuits, because when you offer an employee a "quit or be fired" option, you are probably setting up a "constructive discharge" situation. That is, the employee could still make a claim—for example, of discrimination—against you. Therefore, when allowing an employee to resign instead of be terminated, you should be able to support your actions just as though you were terminating.

Sometimes the issue of unemployment insurance is raised in forced resignations. In most situations, it is possible for the employee to resign and still collect unemployment, and many employers are willing to allow this to happen in the interest of avoiding a termination.

### Reassignment

Might the employee make a worthwhile contribution in another position?

## CONSIDER THE BUSINESS IMPACT OF TERMINATION

If there is a question of the advisability of terminating, consider the following:

You have probably invested a lot in the employee, in time, and in training.

The employee may have valuable contacts that you don't want to lose.

The employee may have specialized knowledge that you cannot easily replace.

There is going to be a period of extra work for you and all your other staff members, plus the training time for a new person.

# DECISION-MAKING FACTORS

What factors should the team take into account when making the decision?

- ❑ How severe the offense is.
- ❑ How clearly the offense is delineated by organization policy and practice.
- ❑ How solid the evidence against the person is.

- ❑ How long the employee has worked for the organization.
- ❑ What the employee's work record shows.
- ❑ How employees committing the same or similar offenses have been treated in the past.
- ❑ The likelihood of a lawsuit.
- ❑ Whether the employee falls into a protected category. And if so, what the employer's record is in hiring and firing other employees in that category.
- ❑ Whether the person has engaged in protected behavior such as taking FMLA leave or whistleblowing.
- ❑ Whether the employee has made any threats of litigation.
- ❑ What the reasonable alternatives are.

## DO TAKE ACTION

If an alternative to termination seems to be the best solution, choose the alternative. But if termination comes out as the best solution, take action.

### Won't the employee take a hint?

It's easy to put a termination off, hoping that things will get better or that the person will "take a hint" and leave. But when you don't act, you are tolerating the behavior, and eventually condoning and accepting it. And all that time, other employees are watching.

A year later, if you finally do terminate, it is harder to show that you really had a rule that you cared about. The employee's attorney will say, "You allowed him to do this for over a year; and now suddenly it's a terminable offense? Perhaps you are fabricating an excuse to cover up discrimination."

# QUIKCHECK

## GROUP DECISION

- ❑ Understand why a group decision is better for the organization.
- ❑ Assemble a group for the decision.

## CONSIDER ALTERNATIVES

- ❑ Suspension without pay.
- ❑ Suspension with pay.
- ❑ "Decision-making" leave.
- ❑ Resignation.
- ❑ Reassignment.

## CONSIDER THE BUSINESS IMPACT

- ❑ Investment in this employee.
- ❑ Contacts and knowledge.
- ❑ Time and disruption.

## MAKE A REASONED DECISION

- ❑ The nature and severity of the offense.
- ❑ The work history of the employee.
- ❑ Actions taken in similar situations in the past.
- ❑ Legal issues.

# STEP 4

# ANSWER THE SIX KEY QUESTIONS

**GOALS FOR STEP 4**

✔*Identify who will be involved, and when and where you will meet.*

✔*Clarify all severence and benefits questions.*

✔*Line up next steps and checkout procedures.*

## WHO WILL BE INVOLVED?

Who should be involved in the termination and what should their roles be?

Terminations are generally conducted by the direct supervisor, although this is not always the case. A representative of the HR department or a higher level manager may have this responsibility.

Others who may be involved include:

- Other managers.
- Representatives of the security department.
- Counselors such as an EAP (employee assistance program) counselor or an outplacement counselor.
- Benefits representatives.

### Consider having two managers present

Many experts recommend having a second manager present during the termination.

With a second manager present, you are assured of a witness to anything said at the termination meeting. Usually, the pair would include the employee's direct supervisor, who would conduct the meeting, as well as an HR professional.

The HR professional is helpful for a number of other reasons, including minimizing risk to the supervisor's safety, and enhancing the credibility of the supervisor conducting the meeting.

The HR professional's presence also affords additional legal protection because he or she can correct any misperceptions or incorrect statements—by either the supervisor or the employee—about the reasons for the discharge or company policy and its application.

A second person is especially advisable if you suspect that your action may cause problems, either in the form of a violent reaction or of a lawsuit.

## WHEN AND WHERE WILL YOU TERMINATE?

Next, decide where and when to hold the meeting.

### When to hold the termination meeting

When should a discharge meeting be conducted? If possible, schedule it near the end of the day.

Select a time that allows the terminated employee to leave the premises with a minimum of embarrassment and to minimize his or her personal contact with other employees when leaving the premises.

Many experts recommend conducting terminations early in the week when possible, so that the employee doesn't immediately face a long weekend, but can get started on the road to a new job right away.

Other experts, on the other hand, recommend terminating on Friday, the idea being that the employee can leave unobstrusively and has the weekend to come to grips with the situation.

You will have to choose the timing that suits your case best.

### Where to conduct the termination

A neutral place like a conference room, out of view of other employees, is usually best.

Many experts advise avoiding using the manager's office; it may be hard to get the employee to leave. The room should be private, with no windows facing work areas, have at least two chairs, and have a desk or a table.

## WHAT SEVERANCE BENEFITS WILL BE OFFERED?

In most terminations, there will be several benefits issues to be discussed with the employee. In the case of upper level managers, the list may be quite extensive.

### Basic benefits review

Review and calculate or obtain the values from the benefits department for the basic benefits coverages. For example:

- ❑ Continuation of various insurances
- ❑ Accrued vacation
- ❑ Accrued sick leave
- ❑ Accrued personal days

**Other kinds of benefits**

Clarify the status of a variety of other benefits, particularly if they have an on-going component.

- ❑ Memberships in professional associations
- ❑ Payments for tuition reimbursement
- ❑ Subscriptions
- ❑ Bonuses
- ❑ Commissions
- ❑ Profit sharing
- ❑ Long term benefits programs such as stock options
- ❑ Relocation-related benefits such as loans and mortgages
- ❑ Company auto
- ❑ Seminars scheduled (appoint a replacement to attend)
- ❑ Civic activities where person represents the organization
- ❑ Scholarships
- ❑ Loans

**Severance pay**

Severance pay is often not given when an employee is discharged for cause. In certain circumstances, however, it may be appropriate, or necessary—if policy requires it, for example—to pay severance to the employee.

☛Severance according to organization policy

Is the employer legally or contractually bound to provide severance?

Does the employer have a written policy, or an unwritten practice, of providing severance? If so, to whom and under what circumstances? Does the employee being fired fit into one of these categories of employees normally awarded severance? If not, what problems and precedents might you create by awarding or not awarding severance? See your HR department.

☛Severance linked to release

There may be cases in which a substantial severance package, coupled with a well-drafted release form, may be the prudent thing to do. Think of it as a form of insurance, one attorney suggests.

Such a release from all future legal claims in exchange for severance pay would probably have to involve additional severance pay beyond that provided for in the organization policy.

Severance packages may be effective lawsuit preventers, especially when you think an employee is very angry and may be in a frame of mind to sue.

The preparation of releases is a job for an attorney. See your HR department for assistance with this task.

### What will the reference state?

If asked, be prepared to clarify what references, if any, the organization will give.

### Payments conditioned on future performance

There may be circumstances in which you need additional work from an employee who is being terminated, for example:

- ❑ Work-in-progress.
- ❑ Additional work expected (review a future report).
- ❑ Briefings to be given.
- ❑ Reports to be filed.

In addition, there may be certain future behaviors that are important to your organization. For example, you may want the person to:

- ❑ Honor a non-compete agreement.
- ❑ Refrain from acting in a manner contrary to the employer's best interest.

In all such cases, you may want to link a future payment to completion of the project, as the employee may not be highly motivated to complete the work otherwise.

# WHAT CHECKOUT STEPS MUST BE FOLLOWED?

The checkout process is difficult in the case of a termination. However, there are often many things to be taken care of, and most are important.

## ITEMS TO GET FROM THE EMPLOYEE

There are probably several items that you need to get from the employee. Many organizations find that a checklist of these items is helpful. Needless to say, once terminated, the employee may not be cooperative in returning items or signing documents.

Here are some of the items companies typically need:

- ❑ ID badges
- ❑ Keys
- ❑ Parking stickers or placards
- ❑ Other security-related items
- ❑ Company credit cards
- ❑ Company-owned tools
- ❑ Computer and associated equipment
- ❑ Cell phone or beeper
- ❑ Other company-owned equipment

## DOCUMENTS AND SIGNATURES TO GET FROM THE EMPLOYEE

- ❑ Signatures on waivers or other documents.
- ❑ Completed forms (including those for continuation or conversion of insurance benefits).

### Legal reminders for the employee

When appropriate, remind departing employees of their obligations under any non-compete, non-solicitation, and non-disclosure agreements, as well as patent, trade secrets and other intellectual property agreements.

Also, mention the penalties for violating such agreements.

### Materials to give to the employee:

You may need to give the employee:

- ❑ Final paycheck (including final pay, as well as any overtime pay, severance pay, accrued vacation and/or sick pay, if applicable).
- ❑ Benefits information.
- ❑ Copy of reference.

### WHAT WILL THE EMPLOYEE'S NEXT STEPS BE?

Is the employee terminated as of the meeting, or do you expect the employee to continue working?

- ☛When will the last day of work be?
- ☛Will the employee go back to his or her office?
- ☛Will the employee be escorted out of the building?
- ☛Will the employee meet with counselors?
- ☛Are there other elements of the checkout routine that must be attended to?

## WHAT SECURITY MEASURES ARE REQUIRED?

Certain situations may require extra security precautions. This should be arranged with security representatives before the termination takes place.

### Situations calling for security

Typically, organizations may want to consider extra security in the following situations:

- ❑ When the possibility of a violent reaction exists.
- ❑ When the possibility of theft is present.
- ❑ When the employee has access to sensitive computer records, programs, or equipment. (Some organizations report that most of their computer problems are not from outside "hackers" but from ex-employees.)
- ❑ When the employee has access to proprietary files such as customer lists.
- ❑ When the employee has access to cash or securities.
- ❑ When the employee has access to trade secrets such as future plans, manufacturing formulas, marketing strategies, etc.
- ❑ Any other time there is a need to protect the property and proprietary rights of the company.

### Typical security precautions

Security precautions may include:

- ☛ Watching the employee remove personal items.
- ☛ Escorting the employee to an exit and/or off the premises.
- ☛ Invalidating the terminated employee's computer password, including e-mail and on-line services.
- ☛ Changing door locks or security codes as necessary.
- ☛ Removing the employee's name as a signatory to any accounts or post office boxes.

### Should the employee be escorted off the premises?

In general, require escorts and other increased security measures only in specified, serious situations. Document guidelines in the policies and procedures handbook.

Employees should never routinely be escorted out of the building by uniformed security guards. Have a valid business reason for using an escort.

When escorting a terminated employee, do it as unobtrusively as possible. An HR professional, or a non-uniformed security official, should be present when the terminated employee is removing personal possessions from the office. Give the employee ample time to gather belongings.

The process of escorting an employee off the premises, unless well-planned and carried out, has potential for charges of defamation, invasion of privacy, intentional infliction of emotional distress, and public humiliation.

## Other considerations

In order to facilitate the employee's departure, consider the following:

☛ Offer to deliver personal property to the employee's residence at company expense.

☛ Offer transportation to get home (or to a previously designated counselor's office or other location).

# QUIKCHECK

## ANSWER THE SIX QUESTIONS

- ❑ Identify all participants in the termination process.
- ❑ Establish when and where the termination will take place.
- ❑ Specify the severance benefits to be offered.
- ❑ Make a list of steps to be followed during the checkout process.
- ❑ Plan the employee's next steps.
- ❑ Arrange for appropriate security measures.

# STEP 5

## ...UGHLY FOR ...N MEETING

**GOALS FOR STEP 5**

✔*Clarify your objectives for the meeting.*

✔*Prepare a step-by-step script for the meeting.*

✔*Perform logistical tasks such as scheduling the meeting and gathering necessary paperwork and supplies.*

No termination will be fun, but if you plan carefully, and you have the materials at hand that you need, you can accomplish it with a minimum of pain and difficulty.

To achieve these results, it's a good idea for the manager who will conduct the termination and the HR representative to have a preparation meeting. This meeting also may appropriately include an outplacement consultant, a counselor from the employee assistance program, and/or other members of the management team.

## CLARIFY YOUR OBJECTIVES

As part of your planning, review the objectives of the termination meeting. In a typical situation, your objectives will be the following:

- ❑ Inform the employee in a straightforward and sensitive manner of three things:
  - —his or her employment is being terminated;
  - —the decision was a corporate, not an individual, decision; and
  - —the decision is final.
- ❑ Provide details of any separation agreement, severance pay, or career transition services.
- ❑ Outline the details of the separation process.
- ❑ Offer support and encouragement.
- ❑ Maintain the employee's dignity and self-esteem.
- ❑ Protect the organization's integrity and image.

## PREPARE A SCRIPT

Since emotions run high during a termination, many managers find it helpful to prepare an outline, or even a script of what they are going to say during the termination.

The next chapter of this book, Step 6—Conduct an Effective Termination, contains a detailed outline of what happens during each of the six phases of the termination meeting. Refer to it when constructing your outline.

# MAKE LOGISTICS ARRANGEMENTS

There are several arrangements you should make to insure that the meeting goes as smoothly as possible.

### Make a formal appointment

Make a formal appointment with the employee. A formal approach is more respectful and less shocking than a casual "Say, do you have a minute?"

### Reserve the space

If you will be using a common space such as conference room, be sure that you have reserved it. You certainly do not want the employee showing up for this meeting, only to find out that the room is in use.

### Check that you have all paperwork

Check to be sure that you have information, documents, checklists, releases for the employee to sign, lists of resources, and so on.

### Check on supplies

Check on tissues, water, paper, pens, and so on.

### Check with other individuals who will participate

Confirm with others who will be at the meeting, or who will be seeing the individual after the termination.

# COMPLETE PERSONAL PREPARATION

In addition to making arrangements, there are personal preparations to be made as well.

### Rehearse the termination

Review your script or outline. Ensure that you are familiar with the separation benefits and services that will be offered.

Many managers find that it is helpful to actually practice saying the words that will be used. This may be done in a role play with an HR representative, a colleague, or possibly an EAP counselor.

## Compose yourself

Just before the meeting, take a few minutes to compose yourself.

Many managers experience feeling resistant, guilty, angry, nervous, compassionate, and/or vulnerable about a termination. These are normal human reactions to a stressful event. Don't be surprised.

Review the reasoning behind the decision to terminate. Be confident that you are doing the right thing, and that you have prepared to do it in the way that is least damaging to the employee.

# QUIKCHECK

## PREPARE THOROUGHLY

- ❑ Clarify the objectives of the termination meeting.
- ❑ Prepare a script or notes of what you will say.
- ❑ Make logistic arrangements.
- ❑ Make a formal appointment.
- ❑ Reserve meeting space.
- ❑ Gather necessary paperwork.
- ❑ Collect necessary supplies.
- ❑ Confirm other participants.
- ❑ Complete personal preparations.
- ❑ Rehearse the termination.
- ❑ Compose yourself.

# STEP 6

# CONDUCT AN EFFECTIVE TERMINATION

**GOALS FOR STEP 6**

✔*Know how to conduct each of the six phases of a termination meeting.*

✔*Understand the importance of following up on questions and on the employee.*

There are six phases to a successful termination meeting. Each phase is presented in detail below, along with tips for handling employee responses.

## PHASE 1. INFORM THE EMPLOYEE

When the employee comes into the office, stand up to greet him or her and then close the door. If possible, sit next to the employee, not behind the desk.

### Be direct

Move directly into the purpose of the meeting. Small talk is inappropriate. The employee is likely to be anxious and deserves to know immediately what is happening.

### Inform of termination and reasons

State that the employee is being terminated and state the reasons for the decision to terminate.

### State the real reasons

It is important to state the real reasons. If you try to "soft-coat" the news by offering some other reason, you are setting yourself up for problems. You will look foolish if you should later try to present the real reasons. For example, don't say, "we have no more work" or "your job has been eliminated," when the real reason is a documented performance failure.

In these situations, the employer usually goes right out and hires a new person to fill the position.

Now the former employee claims wrongful discharge based on discrimination. You told the employee there were no jobs, now you hired to fill the job. Your lame attempts to say, well, it was actually a performance problem, will get nowhere. They will be viewed as a pretext.

If prior warnings have been issued, or if a progressive discipline program has been used, mention that. If goals were agreed to and the employee failed to meet them, say so.

If this is a no-fault situation, you may explain the organization's rationale and what the organization has done to try to make the situation as easy as possible for employees who are being terminated.

### Be clear

Do not be vague. If you are too vague, the employee may not understand that he or she has been fired. Here's an example of a statement that may fail to get the message across:

"Well, times get tough for every company, and this one is no exception, you know, and not everyone can survive the downsizing, do you know what I mean?"

### Avoid platitudes

Avoid statements such as "I know how you feel" or "You will find a new job right away" or "This is really a blessing in disguise." It may be, but this is not the time to try to convince the person of it.

### Examples of termination statements

Here are some examples of direct statements that will be more successful at getting the point across:

"On October 1, you were given a final warning to improve your reliability in making the monthly reports on which we base our materials orders. In addition, we agreed that you were to improve your communication skills with colleagues. Today is January 1. Your reports for October and November were received late and were inaccurate. As a result, shortages and overages have occurred. Furthermore, you have made no apparent effort to communicate more effectively with co-workers. Therefore, we are terminating your employment today."

"As you know, the decision has been made to reduce the company's workforce in light of our present situation. We have analyzed all positions to determine which ones are essential to help us get back on track. As a result of this downsizing and reorganization, your position has been eliminated. No alternative positions are available. Unfortunately, this means that you are being let go, effective immediately."

"As a result of your [failure to follow company regulations, failure to improve your attendance in spite of our series of progressive warnings], the organization has decided to terminate your employment."

Follow-up statements may also be needed, especially in "no-fault" situations. For example:

"I am afraid there are no other alternatives. The decision has been made and it is final. At this time, it is best to understand all the information which has been prepared for you. If you have further concerns, you may contact XXXX to schedule an appointment to discuss this further."

"This was one of the most difficult decisions that this organization has had to make. The action was necessary to bring costs in line and to position the organization for the future."

"This is not a personal decision. The decision is based on the business needs of the organization."

The statements above may seem harsh; however, it is critical that the message be delivered clearly.

## PHASE 2. DEAL WITH EMPLOYEE REACTIONS

Employees may react with anger, sadness, confusion, disbelief, numbness, fear, or a host of other responses. News of the loss of a job affects different people in different ways, sometimes in very surprising and unexpected ways, even in great extremes.

The best advice is to always remain calm and in control, acknowledging the feelings and helping the worker stick to the facts at hand.

Although this period of time may be very uncomfortable, it is important to respect the employee's feelings. A patient and attentive listener will allow the worker to vent frustrations and hostility while sharing anxieties, and this, in turn, will help stem the tide of telephone calls to attorneys.

### WHY I CALLED MY LAWYER

Studies show that the primary reason terminated employees call a lawyer after they've been fired is not for reinstatement, financial restitution, or revenge—but to recapture a sense of dignity they feel has been wrested from them. Especially when terminations are handled poorly, it's no wonder that employees who have lost their jobs often feel overwhelmed and resentful.

It's also important to be prepared, at this point, to answer questions and to have actually rehearsed standard responses. Avoid going beyond these responses, particularly if you are unclear about something, or disagree with a position taken by the employer, or simply don't know the answer. This is where the HR representative, if not the one actually conducting the meeting, might step in to answer questions.

It is fine to acknowledge the employees feelings, and to be generally sympathetic. However, do not agree with any statements the employee makes about, for example, the unfairness of the termination.

Especially important: Do not try to be a psychologist or psychiatrist.

## Typical reactions to termination

Typical employee reactions include the following:

### ☛Normal

The most predictable response to a termination is some showing of hurt and disappointment, and possibly some anger. Most typically, soon after being notified, employees will display passive acceptance and show a normal concern for survival, often asking for help or support. Allow the employee to express feelings. Do not probe too deeply in an attempt to elicit other reactions. The employee may quietly ask a few questions or may remain silent.

**☛Out-of-control**

An out-of-control reaction may indicate serious problems and the need for professional help. In the unlikely event an employee becomes hysterical or violent, stay calm and immediately implement emergency procedures. Tell the worker you will not tolerate violent or aggressive behavior.

Do not get defensive.

Be firm.

Respond with reflection, such as, it sounds like you are very angry.

Do not touch the employee.

**☛Crying and sobbing**

Avoid inane advice such as, it's not that important.

Let the person cry. Offer tissues and water.

When composure is regained, continue.

**☛Controlled**

Occasionally an employee may react as if this were "no big deal." Ask clarifying questions to ensure that the information was actually heard and understood. However, do not invade the person's privacy with a question such as, do you understand the impact this will have on your family?

**☛Shocked**

Lack of any reaction at all is a danger signal. It may be useful to test whether the person has gotten the message by saying, "Do you understand what I'm saying?" If the person doesn't, then repeat the termination statement, paraphrase it, or expand on it if possible.

The employee may need additional time for feelings and responses to surface.

## Phase 3. Lay out the terms

Once the person seems clear about the decision, go ahead with an explanation of the separation package, if there is one. Here is one example of what you might say.

"In an effort to assist you financially, we have put together a separation package that includes severance pay. [The benefits manager] is waiting to explain the severance and other benefits to you. [Or, the severance package includes the following... ]

We also have arranged for outplacement assistance; this is a service designed to assist you in a career development analysis and your job search efforts. A consultant is here today to answer your questions about outplacement and to set up a schedule for future meetings. [or, an appointment has been made for ... , or the counselor may be reached at this number ...] I encourage you to take advantage of all the services being offered."

At this point, it is useful to hand the employee a packet of materials that delineates the benefits and separation package and includes names and phone numbers for additional information.

Make any reminders necessary with regard to trade secret, non-compete, and other similar agreements.

## Phase 4. Let the employee know what's next

Now let the employee know what will be required next.

First, discuss what needs to be done with the logistics of the departure—vacating the office, packing up personal materials, returning property, exit interview, meeting with counselor, etc.

Be clear who—the HR representatives, the EAP counselor, the supervisor—will perform checkout responsibilities, such as collecting keys, credit cards, etc., and when this will happen.

If the list of things to do or people to see is extensive, hand the employee a list or schedule.

If the employee is to be escorted during the departure, mention this.

If the employee is to continue working for some period, clarify the organization's expectations for this period.

## Phase 5. Answer employee questions

Ask if the employee has any questions, and, if so, answer them. If you don't know the answer, say so and tell the employee you will get back with the answer.

In general, answer (or find an answer to) questions about benefits, ongoing assignments, checkout procedures, outplacement, paycheck, etc.

In general, do not answer questions about the reasons for the firing, or its appropriateness except by repeating the initial comments.

### Avoid debating with the employee

Avoid debating or bargaining with the employee. If the employee brings up a genuine question relating to benefits, you might agree or say that you will contact human resources and let the person know.

For example, the person might ask to keep home office equipment for a few weeks until other arrangements can be made. Or an employee might state that extra severance pay would be fair because he or she worked for the organization as an independent contractor for two years before joining the organization. If granting such requests would avoid a lawsuit and encourage the person to speak well of the organization, it is probably in the organization's best interest to grant them.

### Avoid discussing other employees

Avoid discussing severance or termination agreements that have been reached with other employees.

However, if the employee has a valid point that suggests that he or she was treated unfairly in comparison with other employees, you may want to agree to talk to the HR department.

For example, if the employee states, correctly, that everyone else let go in similar circumstances has been allowed to continue a certain benefit, you might want to consider, for consistency's sake, allowing this employee the same benefit.

### Don't be defensive

Resist trying to defend the organization and its decisions. If you have the right reasons for termination and have documented those reasons, you have no reason to be defensive.

Avoid angry, inappropriate, or illegal statements.

Avoid giving the employee advice.

## Phase 6. Conclude the Meeting

Remember, the termination meeting should be brief—no more than 10-15 minutes.

When the employee has finished asking questions and seems reasonably composed, close the meeting.

Rise from your seat, which will cue the employee to do the same, and accompany the employee to the person who will be handling the next stage of the process.

If appropriate, make a supportive closing statement such as "I appreciate the contributions you have made here and if I can be of any assistance, please let me know."

# FOLLOW UP AS NEEDED

When the employee walks out the door, you may heave a sigh of relief, but your job is not done. Here is what to do next.

### Document the meeting

Write a memo summarizing the meeting and send it to the HR department for placement in the employee's file. Note what you said and what the employee said. In particular, note any inflammatory statements or threats to sue by the employee, along with any admissions that could be used to defend against a later claim of wrongful discharge.

### Follow up on questions

If the employee asked any questions during the termination meeting that you could not answer, get answers or get the appropriate expert to work on the answers. Follow up to be sure that the information gets to the terminated employee.

### Follow up on the employee

Check to be sure that the employee followed through with the list of things to do and people to see. Were all materials turned in? Were appointments kept?

### Conduct an exit interview if appropriate

Exit interviews may be appropriate for many termination situations. See Appendix B for information about exit interviewing after terminations.

### Notify customers, clients, receptionists

Make any notifications necessary, including your customers, contacts, receptionist, phone answerers, and so on.

Let them know that the individual is no longer with the organization, and give them details about whom to call and what arrangements have been made concerning on-going projects, major orders, and so on.

Certainly top customers and contacts should not be greeted with, "Oh, she's left the organization. Is there anyone else who can help you?"

Even worse, perhaps, would be a similar message on voicemail.

### Maintain confidentiality

Confidentiality and privacy are very important at termination time. Everyone involved in the termination must maintain strict confidentiality.

Maintain "need-to-know." Keep a strict need-to-know policy for all information related to the separation(s). After the terminated employee has left, the circumstances surrounding the employee's termination should remain confidential, with only those managers who have "a need to know" brought into the information loop. Co-workers, customers, and others should merely be told that the employee no longer works at the company.

Employees who push for more information should be told that, "As you know, I just can't discuss private personnel matters. Company policy is very strict on that."

## YOU ARE DONE

If you have reached this spot in the book, your termination is completed. Having followed the steps outlined in this book, you have made the job as easy on yourself as possible, and you have preserved the dignity of the employee as well. Finally, you have reduced to a minimum the possibility of a lawsuit.

## WELL DONE.

# QUIKCHECK

## CONDUCT AN EFFECTIVE TERMINATION

- ❑ Keep the meeting short.
- ❑ Follow the script.
- ❑ Inform the employee.
- ❑ Deal with the employee's reaction.
- ❑ Lay out the terms of the separation.
- ❑ Let the employee know what is next.
- ❑ Answer the employee's questions.
- ❑ Conclude the meeting.

## FOLLOW UP AS NEEDED

- ❑ Document the meeting.
- ❑ Follow up on questions.
- ❑ Make apropriate notifications to customers, clients, and so on.
- ❑ Maintain confidentiality.

# APPENDIX A

## TRAINER'S GUIDE

There are a variety of ways in which this book can be incorporated into supervisory and managerial training programs.

### YOUR PREPARATION

Whatever method of presentation you use, you will have to do some preparation yourself.

#### 1. Get to know the book and its concepts

To use this book as a training tool, you must familiarize yourself with this book and basic steps in a termination.

#### 2. Relate to your organization

To provide the most effective training, connect the concepts in the book with the operations of your organization.

- ☛ Review your organization policies and determine which need to be presented. Be sure to include severance and related benefits policies.
- ☛ Review your organization's employee handbook to see what policies need to be mentioned or referred to.

- ☛ Collect any forms or checklists your organization uses for terminations.
- ☛ Think through your state laws and how to fit that information into the training.
- ☛ Review lawsuits and charges brought against your organization as a result of terminations. Use these to build your presentation. (You probably do not want to discuss actual cases, or use real names.)
- ☛ If your industry has special rules, plan how to integrate them into the training.

**3. Select a method of presentation**

How will you present the QuikStep Firing material? One quick session? Several longer sessions? Eight sessions spread out over eight months?

There are many approaches to presenting training; you must decide which one will work best for your organization. The suggestions which follow will assist you.

☛Let the book do the training

The simplest approach is to hand out this book, ask managers to read it, and then hold a discussion period during a regularly-scheduled managers' meeting or special meeting just for this purpose. During the discussion, managers may comment on the book and ask follow-up questions

If you choose this method, be sure to schedule a time at a future meeting for managers to comment on the book or ask questions.

☛Single session

The next level of training would be to schedule a single session of one to two hours on the issues raised in the book. The meeting would include a presentation and discussion of the concepts; perhaps a role play, and time for specific examples and materials from your organization.

There are two approaches to this session: having the participants read the book before attending the training, or having them read it after the session.

**Read the book beforehand.** In this case you will review the concepts, answer questions, discuss applications, and provide specific information about your organization's policies and practices, and your experiences with past lawsuits.

**Read the book afterwards.** With this approach, you will present the concepts at one meeting, and have your managers read the book on their own.

This will be most effective if you schedule a follow-up session at which managers share their reactions to the book and ask questions.

## Suggested outline—single session

- ❑ Every supervisor and manager will have to terminate employees.
- ❑ This is a difficult duty, and many managers do it poorly because of lack of preparation.
- ❑ Terminations trigger lawsuits.
- ❑ Go over the steps one by one, answering questions as you go.
- ❑ Cover any special aspects involving your organization's business, special policies, or special problems.

## Suggested outline—several sessions

The most effective training is accomplished over a period of time. For example, spend the first fifteen minutes of each monthly management meeting on this training, following a schedule similar to the one presented below.

### First Meeting —Why this is important

Introduce the book with the questions about the firing process and difficulties employees have with it. What can go wrong? What are the consequences of a poorly-handled termination?

If your organization has had lawsuits or morale problems related to firings, discuss them.

### Intermediate Meetings—Cover the steps one-by-one

Since some of the steps are more detailed than others, you probably won't need the same amount of time for each step. Three to five meetings should be plenty.

### Final Meeting

Review the steps.

Take the attendees through a mock termination. Set up a termination situation that is typical of your organization. Have participants role play the steps.

If you wish all attendees to role play a termination, schedule extra time.

Allow some time to answer participants' questions.

## SUCCESSFUL TRAINING

Be sure that you follow the basics of good training: conduct the training in a comfortable setting, free from interruptions. Be sure that all required equipment and materials are in place. Arrange for refreshments if appropriate.

Managers who follow the principles in this book will be successful at making terminations. It is the trainer's job to be sure the managers study the principles, understand them, and know the situations in which they apply.